INSPIRATIONS OF THE
HEART

SPIRITUAL SONGS, POEMS AND INSPIRATIONALS

William P. Santos

Copyright © 2024 **William P. Santos Publishing**

All rights reserved. No part of this publication may be reproduced, distributed, or transmitted in any form or by any means, including photocopying, recording, or other electronic or mechanical methods, without the prior written permission of the publisher, except in the case of brief quotations embodied in critical reviews and certain other noncommercial uses permitted by copyright law. For permission requests, write to the publisher, addressed "Attention: Book Rights and Permission," at the address below.

Published in the United States of America

ISBN 978-1-963379-17-4 (SC)

William P. Santos Publishing
222 West 6th Street
Suite 400, San Pedro, CA, 90731
williampls48@gmail.com

Ordering Information and Rights Permission:

Quantity sales. Special discounts might be available on quantity purchases by corporations, associations, and others. For details, contact the publisher at the address above.

For Book Rights Adaptation and other Rights Permission. Call us at toll-free 1-888-945-8513 or send us an email at admin@stellarliterary.com.

CONTENTS

FORWARD viii
INTRODUCTION POEM x
IN MY OWN WORDS BY WILLIAM P. SANTOS xi

LONELINESS 1
I WANT TO LIVE... 3
THERE IS NO BETTER LOVE 6
DAD WHERE WERE YOU... 9
A KNOCKING SOUND 11
THE PEN OF THE WRITER 14
RAINBOW OF PROMISE 16
VISITING THE GARDEN 18
TRUE GLORY 20
BE YOURSELF 22
WHAT WE CAN AND CAN'T DO 24
CREATIONS FORMAT 26
ADOLESCENTS 30
TIME CONTINUES ON 12/13/08. 32
THE BROKEN RIBBON 34
THE LOST NATION 35
LORD WHAT YOU ARE TO ME. 37
LORD, YOU SMILE AT ME... 38
THE WEIGHT OF A DREAM 39
THEIR GOING TO LIVE WITH ME 42
IT IS MY DESIRE TO KNOW YOU 44
INFUSE ME WITH STRENGTH 47
WHEN YOU DIE, WHAT LIFE FORM WILL YOU BE? 49
REMEMBER ME 51
REMEMBER CHRIST BY REMEMBERING OTHERS 52

IN TIMES OF TROUBLE	53
MODEL OF A MAN	55
MODEL OF A WOMAN	57
THE PAST	59
IT'S AMAZING	60
THE TREE THAT WITHERED	63
WHAT CAME FIRST THE CHICKEN OR THE EGG?	65

INSPIRATIONS OF THE HEART

BY

WILLIAM SANTOS

THIS IS A BOOK OF POETRY AT IT'S BEST. FEATURING , **I WANT TO LIVE.** A HEART MOVING POEM ON ABORTION. SONGS AND INSPIRATIONAL WRITINGS THAT WARM THE SOUL. READ ON AND BE BLESSED.

INSPIRATIONS OF THE HEART

Spiritual poems, songs, devotionals and Inspirational

Topics. Take up your cross
And follow me!

FORWARD

Poetic inspiration is the expression of the soul. Some expressions are naturally inspired, and some are supernaturally inspired. But for the most part, poetry is communication by creatively processing one's thoughts and translating those thoughts in a manner that appears to be with graceful eloquence and is often enigmatic. Poetry is the perception of one's life and surroundings and often explains the environment in which the inspired poem was developed. Poetry also manifests a different perspective for it describes the deep-rooted emotional content of one's mindset at the time pen met paper.

This book of poetry is an epic compilation of various spiritually motivational poems, songs, and inspirational writings that entail deep pondering and meditation of the heart. They are supernaturally inspired by the very prompting of God's Holy Spirit as he spoke ever so gently to my heart in a still small voice. I know this because at times I experienced writer's block and only when God filled my mind with inspiration could I write these words of grace.

Now each person has a different manner in which they express their emotions. Instead of venting on people I chose to write mine through poetry, songs, and inspirational writings, which reveal how I was delivered through the present trying circumstances.

<u>1 Corinthians 10:13</u> (There hath no temptation taken you, but such as is common to man; but god is faithful, who will not suffer you to be tempted above that ye are able: but will with the temptation also make a way to escape, that ye may be able to bear it.)

Writing these poems, songs, and inspirational writings was God's Avenue of helping me to escape waddling in the temptations of depression and despair, anxiety and hopelessness, and the smoky surroundings of my temporary depraved condition.

Just as Paul the Apostle was bound and in chains, I experienced bondage and affliction. And yet in these difficult conditions, we experience certain similarities of depression, anxiety, loneliness, rejection, fear, doubt, confusion, and gloom, in whichever emotional state one may be in, the comforting Holy Spirit is able to comfort us and give us a peace of mind, wherein the fruition of poetry will flow from the soul, and it is this fruit that I bestow unto you.

These poems, songs, devotionals, and inspirational topics contain the true spiritual riches that God intended for us to possess; wisdom, knowledge, understanding, faith, hope, and love. Many of the concepts are scripturally oriented, but all are authentic and of Holy Spirit descent.

I pray that you are encouraged, inspired, and blessed from the highest. Read on and get enveloped in the deep concepts and healing words that give new meaning to life, as well as reveal the hidden treasures of Inspirations of the Heart.

INTRODUCTION POEM

I pray this book appeal to your heart, to read what lies within its seal,

And as you continue to read to obtain its riches, you will find the inspirations are o so real.

I was cast into the sea, drifted from coast to coast, confined within a shell,

Thus come these poems, the fruit sorrow yielded, even while the tempest tossed and the billows swell.

Ordained to uplift the weary, broken hearted with eyes tired and teary,

And those with dreams that seem to fade, because hope seems to be a distant query.

I pray that you are inspired and moved with passion to walk this narrow road,

For at the end you will find peace, and all the love that God bestowed.

IN MY OWN WORDS
BY WILLIAM P. SANTOS

This is a book of poetry at its best. Featuring, <u>I Want to Live</u>. A heart-moving poem on abortion, with a creative flare and perspective of an unborn child. It's saturated with heart-moving songs and inspiring inspirational writings that will warm your soul and motivate you to be more spiritually minded. The poems tend to take on the personality of many abstract objects and express new perspectives that can only be grasped if one imagines that they are one with the object. Jesus himself used similar techniques of communication, taking cryptic, enigmatic messages and using simple abstract objects such as the tree that withered, to bring understanding to the common individual.

Shut your eyes and imagine you are a pen. Picture what your purpose in life as a pen is. Now would you desire your ink to dry up, or desire to be placed in motion, knowing that when you let the ink go, it will last for a lifetime, causing peace or strife, death or life, leaving eternal impressions on the mind of all who read its content. But if you hold the ink, it will dry up leaving nothing behind but a hardened core wrapped in hard plastic or a thin metal casing. What would you say if you were that pen and had a voice? This is where <u>The Pen of the Writer</u> came from. I placed myself in the very heart of the pen, the core which is the ink and what it was designed for and gave the pen a voice.

Try indwelling the words of these poems, grasp their depth and you will be edified. See if you can see what I see through my eyes. Not the ones that blink, the ones that think, the inner ones that can only be seen when I jot them down in ink.

LONELINESS

Have you ever felt an emptiness or a void in your life so big that you Felt like nothing could fill it except a certain person or thing? You've longed for them or it for so long, or it was taken away from you and now you don't know what to do. So now you're trying to fill it with someone else or something else, like wild parties, drugs, and drinking, yet still, that emptiness persists and continues to grow like the deepest abyss. You feel lost out at sea with no captain, the billows continue to swell, the tempest continues to blow, the current of your emotions take you every which way the waves go, back and forth, and you can't rest. You want the waves to calm and the sun to stop beating upon your head and chest, instead, you thirst and you long to quench it with that person or thing. You've asked the Lord "Why me, why do I have to go through such torment and pain, why can't you just heal my heart by granting my request", and so you question why that void exists?

Can you see any other way for God to get your attention? You couldn't draw closer to him because you always had someone or something else in the way. You wouldn't even talk to him had you had that person or thing in your life, you would feel like they sustain you and that you had everything you needed in life and would've overlooked the most important element and essential, God. He longs for your attention, he wanted to speak with you, but you never gave him the time of day. When that person called you jumped to your feet, but when God called… you paused, heard, and went your merry way ignoring that still small voice that had been calling you since you were born, the one that spoke to you ever so softly while you were still in your mother's womb.

God said, "Behold, I stand at the door and knock: if any man hears my voice, and opens the door, I will come into him and will sup with him, and he with me". Revelations 3:20

Likewise, when God stands at the door of your heart, knocking and knocking, we often treat him like a peddler, someone trying to sell us something. Yet on the contrary, he's not trying to sell us something, he's trying to give us something, his love, his peace, his joy, and all his riches in glory. Why not open the door of your heart, and receive his love, his peace of mind, and his joy that no man or thing can take away from you?

I WANT TO LIVE.

Roe vs. Wade, the case of free will to kill one's unborn child. In every case according to our constitutional rights, we have the right to a fair trial, with a jury of our peers. We have the right to testify in our defense. But who is truly on trial? Can you point out the defendant in the courtroom? Who is the one receiving the death sentence? Who would take the stand if they could and say, "I want to live"? He or she wants a jury of their peers because their rights are being violated, and he or she is being condemned without a voice. What would those peers say during deliberation? Hear their verdict, there are millions of them waiting to speak, or should I say were.

I saw a picture of a twelve-week-old fetus (baby, human) It had just been aborted and there was a pile of ground-up body parts, with fully developed hands and feet sticking out in the middle. It looked the same as the destruction from a terrorist bombing. What's the difference? There is no difference. Who are we to play God saying who should live and who should die?

This poem is written from the perspective of an unborn child. I thought what would they say in their defense? What would they say about abortion? When a person is being put to death, we ask him if he has any last words. What about the unborn? What if they could speak, what would they say in their defense? Sometimes we never consider if we were that child being exterminated before having a chance to speak or a chance to defend ourselves. We often forget that we once began as an embryo and fetus, to a newborn, to a young child, to adolescence onto adulthood. Who determines at what stage you should die? Well, hear what this unborn child says.

I want to live! But they say I have no choice in the matter,

I'm just an embryo, who fell short of a fetus because my life was shattered. My mom thought she would yield to the sad song of pro-choice,

I wish I could speak, but if I could, would they hear my voice?

Mom thought I was like a preservative she could place aside upon a shelf;

did she love me too much to let me be born, or was she just loving herself?

She thought maybe later, when life is good, she'll be ready to have another, but when later came, instead of having a little girl, it was my baby brother.

One day I would like to ride a bike, roller skate, can you relate?

Who was you mom to end my destiny, God blessing me, now what's my fate?

Long ago babies felt secure resting inside their mother womb,

but now millions are being terminated inside this dreaded tomb.

Mom let me have the chance to laugh or cry and experience gloom,

for I was like a flower but you plucked me before I could bloom.

I'm like a bird with wings, but never knew what it was like to fly,

Mom let the Lord make the decision of whether I live or whether I die.

I want to live, but why would you rather me die?

Are you to afraid of me being born and looking into my eyes?

I would probably resemble you, having such a beautiful smile,

But instead, I was condemned to death without even having a fair trial.

What if you were me, looking to your mom for love and protection,

But instead found yourself feeling the hate and rejection.

I'm like a baseball player who can't play for lack of a glove,

I'm like a broken heart, cracked for the lack of love.

I'm like an egg, destined to be an eagle, but only became a yoke,

I'm like a precious plant, in it's early stages that a weed came up to choke.

I'm like an astronaut, who never flew into space or to the moon,

I'm like an instrument that never played a single tune.

I'm like a tree, hoping one day for the world to taste of my fruit,

So sweet, yet never came to past, because I was plucked up by the root.

I felt a vacuum tube up inside tearing me apart,

My limbs, my body, and then it sucked out my heart.

I leaped, I jumped, but there was no were for me to hide,

Why are they doing this ruthless deed; to ensure I die.

I want to live, but it I'm not old enough to have a say,

I know everyone must die, but my mom determined my time today.

Mom, maybe I was destined to be a lawyer or doctor to help you stand, instead you terminated me, even before I had the chance to hold your hand.

8/22/01

THERE IS NO BETTER LOVE

Some believe in love at first sight. They can remember the first time that they laid eyes on the one they fell in love with. Some are still together to this day, and others are not so fortunate. Somehow that love faded, why, I don't know, but maybe it was not love to begin with, maybe it was just infatuation or fickle love. Real love has very distinguishable traits, it's patient, slow to speak, slow to wrath, and quick to listen. It bears all things, believes all things, hopes all things, and endures all things. Real love is unconditional, not based on circumstances, it's for richer or poorer, sickness and health. Well God loved us at first sight, and he loves us unconditionally. He loved us before we were even created, even with his foreknowledge, knowing that we would sin and fall short of his standard. And because of his foreknowledge he prepared a way beforehand to reconcile our relationship back with him even before we broke it. You have to prepare your mind for the worst situation and ask yourself, can I love them through that? If not, you don't have real love. There is no better love than God's. Read the words of this song.

There is no better love than what Jesus gave,

No better love than what he displayed.

Oh what better love, can you receive,

There is but one love that you can believe.

I was broken hearted, discouraged and dismayed,

Needed someone to comfort me and come to my aid.

Was so confused, and almost went astray,

Then Jesus came and rescued me and showed me the way.

Vamp:

It would have been me, who was still lost,

It should have been me hanging on that old cross.

With nails in my hands and in my feet,

But it was the love of Jesus that wouldn't let that be.

No other love would lay down and die,

No other love would give up it's own life.

It's the only love you can't define,

For it goes beyond the comprehension of the mind.

Vs 2.

I sought for true love an couldn't find it anywhere

Was looking for someone special hoping they would care.

There was emptiness inside and I didn't know what to do,

So I called unto Jesus and said I fond this love in you.

Lord I know your love, is a love that's real,

It's not a superficial, only focused on the outward appeal.

But you were there for me, looking pass my sinful deeds,

Washed me with your blood, and met all my needs.

Vamp:

It would have been me, who was still lost,

It should have been me, hanging on that old cross.

With nails in my hands and in my feet,

But it was your love for me that wouldn't let that be.

No other love, would lay down and die,

No other love, would give up it's own life.

It's the only love you can't define,

For its Jesus love that bled from his side.

It would have been me, hit in my face,

It would have been me, but you took my place.

I would've been dead, but you gave me life,

Only a real love would make such a sacrifice.

Thank you Lord, for redeeming me,

Breaking my chains and setting me free.

There's no better love than what Jesus gave,

There is no better love than what he displayed.

DAD WHERE WERE YOU

More and more people today are growing up without a father in the home. Mom and Dad either separated or got divorced, and the children are wondering, "Where is dad or mom and why aren't they at home?" They can't comprehend excuses. They think that no circumstance should cause them to grow up without a father. Well, I did. I grew up without a father in the home and this is what I wrote.

Dad, throughout my life I had many trials, many frowns many smiles.

Many letters from you heaped up in trash piles. But as I look back in retrospect, to collect the memories I regret, I see your face, what a waste of a father out of his place. Where were you? As I would reminisce of who I would miss, who at times would have me clinching my fist, it was you, where were you? What role did you play in my life; every thought of you was like being pierced with along jagged knife: ripping ever so deeply down into my soul, just thinking of how you have forsaken your fatherly role. Dad where were you?

Where were you when mom enrolled me into school, when my peers influenced me to be cool, saying I had to break a rule. But I learned the hard way by getting expelled from school; I guess I was a fool. Dad, where were you? Where were you when they taught me to read, I wanted you to take the lead, hoping you would plant your seed, for I sprouted up like a plant but got choked by a weed. The plant was my hopes, the weed was greed, was it greed that took you away from me? Dad, where were you?

I remember the time I ran my first race, the goal was at my fingertips so close I could taste first place, But I lost my pace thinking of your face. Discouraged, I fell with my head hung low; thinking not having a father was a very low blow. Dad, where were you? Where were you when I got in my first fight, I would have walked away but I thought of you and through a left and a right. I later got in trouble and had to run, O boy went and got a gun, so I thought I'd better get one. I needed your advice from father to a son, I looked for a real friend, but I didn't have one. Where were you pops? Where are you now that I'm running from the cops?

Many of nights I've cried, wondering if you had died, but now my tears have dried, and my eyes are open wide No longer hearing your voice inside. It's like a broken radio and all I hear is fuzz, cause if you were to ask me why, I would tell you because I want to be the father that you never was.

A KNOCKING SOUND

Have you ever feared reading a book that contained information about the devil? Or have you ever feared encountering a spirit or ghost? Well before I knew that the Devil possessed no power except it be given from above, then I felt my mind was playing tricks on me. I used to read the Bible all the way through and when I came to Revelation, I would close the Bible. Why? Because I was afraid of hearing about the Devil and demons, and also because I heard many horror stories about people seeing ghosts and departed loved ones. But one day I felt brave and desired to read it. Now let me inform you of one thing, at the time I read this, I neither believed in seeing ghosts or spirits, my opinion was that the people who said they saw spirits probably were either on drugs or they were hallucinating. Yet as it may be, my poem will explain what happened. Read on and be comforted that God is in control of everything, everybody, and even every spirit and that no spirit or person or thing can harm one hair on your head without God allowing it. And if he allows it, know that everything works together for the good of them that love God, to them that are the called according to his purpose. So read and be encouraged.

I sat upon a chair to read late one ebony night,

'Twas dim and cozy under my flickering candlelight.

Thought I heard a knock, so I haste unto the door,

I opened, just saw Glimmering Street lights, nothing more.

Opening my Bible once again, exploring Revelation,

Yet this time fear overwhelmed me with an ire sensation.

Again a knocking sound, I wondered what it be,

Curious I opened, vaguely seeing a white cat fleeing away from me.

Stunned, I shut the door in shock of what I saw,

A cat doesn't have rapping knuckles, only scratching claws.

And why did it vanish just halfway across my grass,

Was it an evil spirit, or just that blazing fast.

The more I read it seemed to only get worse,

I never saw a spirit, would Revelation be a blessing or a curse.

I closed my Bible and pondered, the more I read they draw near,

I was so hesitant to reopen, not knowing what spirit might appear.

Once again a knocking sound, only this time I slowly opened,

'Twas the cat from across the street hungry for a stroking.

Yet never before he knocked, nor was he white,

Not pale like the ghostly cat that vanished from my sight.

For a season I paused to read, for fear of the knocking,

I needed strength to move on, So I tried mentally blocking.

Then I read the book of Job, and I saw Satan appealing,

To God for he had no power and this calm my feelings.

Once again I opened Revelations, persistent I read it through,

I saw the blessing not a curse, my superstitions were not true.

Satisfied from what I read, I only hear the ticking of my clock,

No more visitations in the night, not as much as an ire knock.

THE PEN OF THE WRITER

The pen though just a plastic, metallic, or wooden tube filled with ink or even compressed in a feather can be a very useful item. The Bible says the pen is mightier than the sword. Meaning it is more awesome and imposing. You can impress people more with a pen than with a sword. How is that? Well, the pen is a mere reflection of the mind and soul of mankind. The Bible was written with a pen reflecting the mere mind of God. When we write it is the transparency of the soul, the mind, the will, and the emotions of the inner being. Words can reflect anger or joy, the pen was designed not to have an opinion or to be objective, it was only designed to be used, it doesn't care. Well, hear the voice of a pen in this poem.

The Pen of the Writer had one sole desire,

That was to be used when the author felt inspired.

Then the ink would flow leaving words of inspiration,

feeding food for thought and fruitful contemplation.

With no mixed emotions only writing what was thought,

The language didn't matter to spew ink is what it sought.

But poetry was its passion the renaissance of literary art,

relaying cryptic messages from an inspired poet's heart.

If the author was inspired with words from up above,

The pen of the writer would record words of love.

But if the writer was dejected and in an angered state,

The pen would follow suit jotting down words of hate.

Now if the author was jubilant and experienced brighter days,

His heart would then rejoice as the pen inscribed the praise.

With the flare of calligraphy, the elegant penmanship prance,

reflecting the writers gracefulness as he made that pen dance.

But all too often retired is the pen that desires to write,

waiting to be an influence under a radiant candlelight.

The pen's mightier than the sword and can vanquish the modern Nero,

With the signature of a provost ruler, who decided to make ink the uncommon hero.

Putting ends to wars for the pen is more than a thing,

It could be used for world peace or to empower an arrogant king.

Come says he, lets make history, our future is on the brink,

Let me make love to paper while you write whatever you think.

RAINBOW OF PROMISE

Times may be rough sometimes, but we know it will not last always. God said that those who live Godly will suffer persecution and that we would be tried. But we know that tribulation works with patience, and when we learn what it is that God is trying to teach us and take it patiently, the problem will almost always subside, unless God says, my grace is sufficient.

But even in that case, all is well and you must remember God's promises, just as he left his rainbow to remind us that the world would not be flooded again. So read this poem and let it saturate your soul with hope, for God cares for you.

Though I feel the chill's of fear running down my spine,

The Lord has turned the later rain into the promise of sunshine.

His bow can be seen when the storms of life subside,

Reflecting His mercy when the water and light collides.

How can we take for granted such a wonderful beautiful gift,

Lord help us to remain faithful and never to stray or drift.

I will always remember just how you let the world know,

The Love you bestowed through the ark of a colorful rainbow.

Lord I'm very, very grateful and always will be,

Thankful for your love and tender mercy.

If it had not been for you what would I do,

O Lord what would I do for I could not make it through.

What greater way to make your love show,

Than create awe and beauty through a colorful rainbow.

Your promise to us to never destroy by flood again,

But yet atone for the sins of all mortal men.

Just claim it by faith for the bow reflects Jesus face,

Climb it and you will be in a heavenly place.

Climb the ark of Gods love my friend climb,

Until you reach the top press on and do not resign.

VISITING THE GARDEN

      Think of the most beautiful places on the planet that you ever visited or heard of, or seen in pictures. Think of the clarity of the water, the color of the reef, the plant life, and its flora design. Think of the horizons and the whole spectrum of animal life, and how different it is all over the world. Well combine every place in the world from Europe to Asia and Africa to Australia, Antarctica to the North Pole and you would only have a mere glimpse of the Garden of Eden. Noting in this present age can compare to the Garden of Eden. The air and quality of mineral water were so pure back then, the vegetation was more flourishing, and animal life was massive, vibrant, and healthy. A Lion today would probably look like a kitten compared to a lion back then. There was no pollution or smog, no contaminated water, you could just go to the nearest stream and drink the most crystal clear, thirst-quenching drink you've ever drank. Read this poem and envision yourself amid the Original Garden of Eden.

I often wondered of Eden, the most beautifully arrayed garden,

Oh how I wanted to see it, if only the Lord would grant me a pardon.

One day I was daydreaming, and drifted into a semiconscious trance,

I found myself in the midst of the Garden, as the Lord gave me a mere glance.

There was peace without confusion, of modern day propaganda,

Animals living in perfect harmony, like the lion, the lamb and panda.

Tree's withered not, nor did flowers lose their lustrous array,

God's glory filled the garden, of his ultimate kingdom plantae.

There was fruit-bearing tree's, many sorts of every type and kind,

Some so luscious looking, they tantalized my curious mind.

There were herbs of every sort, yet there were no choking weeds,

We didn't lack a thing, for God was its gardener and supplied our every need.

I was mesmerized; the architecture was a masterpiece 'twas brilliant,

Gods glory so superior, and his power far beyond resilient.

The work so spectacular, it commanded your undivided attention,

Each element was so intricate, like being in a whole new dimension.

The ground was rich with minerals; the river's crystal clear,

The environment seemed perpetual, and utterly free from fear.

There was pure gold, bdellium, and the precious onyx stone,

There was luminous colors reflecting through the atmospheres Ozone.

There were four rivers, Pison, Gihon, hiddekel and the Euphrates,

And as you looked up to the heavens you could see more stars than just the Pleiades.

I was satiated for I had seen perfection, and oh what a great sensation,

I just lifted my hands in praise and offered the creator a standing ovation.

I could dream on forever, and wish to extend my stay,

And find my self in awe, daydreaming of the garden day after day.

So I pray, and thank the Lord for granting me a wonderful pardon,

And look forward to the new paradise, when I will view heavens garden.

TRUE GLORY

What is true glory? Some think it's when you make it to the top in the eyes of the world, but this glory fades. Look a Michael Jackson, Mike Tyson, and Michael Jordan, where is their glory now? It is fading, and now that glory is being passed on to another. But what about real true glory, it remains, just look up at the sky and the stars, see the horizons, and tell me have they faded? Or does their glory remain? The Bible says the heavens declare the glory of God. Scientists and evolutionists try to discredit God, coming up with some demented Idea that all things we now see were developed over a period of time, evolving out of something that was not. When was the last time you saw something come from nothing? The same elements: water, oxygen, and some sort of mineral or food source sustain all life. Eliminate one of the three elements and all physical life would come to an end.

So, as you read this poem, let it remind you to look up each day and see the true glory that does not fade, and you will see the one to be glorified, God! All glory goes to him because he sustains it all and will change it all, rearrange it all, and in the end, you will see true glory.

As I rise each day, to view heavens glorious array,

Just the way God established its glory in his own special way.

And all he had to do is say, let there be light and the stars would portray,

His glory, even the clouds whether black, white or gray.

True glory is when you can say sun rule the day, and moon at night,
Airs oscillate and lift the birds up in flight that's their plight.
Sonar guide bats so they can fly when they have no light,
Snakes have inferred so you can see what you strike.

How can a shark sense a blood drop from two miles away?
How did God create all beings from one lump of clay?
How does he tell the sea to stay and it obeys?
Why has the sun not fizzled out and we feel sunrays?

That's true glory and it belongs to God.

BE YOURSELF

Now is the time when there are more plastic surgeons than pediatricians, and why is that? People are trying to look like someone else and act like someone else. They no longer like themselves and so they try to change their appearance, and their actions, trying to be fussily prim and prissy around the rich and famous, or thuggish and gangster in the hood so as to not look vulnerable and weak. Losing their identity and hide behind a mask of different personalities, and personalities they feel will be accepted by their peers.

If we were in a world where there was only one type of flower and that flower only came in one color, this would not be a very colorful world.

Who can add one cubit to their stature? God did not make us all identical; he made us different for a reason. Accept who you are in Christ Jesus, and you will be satisfied with what you look like. It's not your looks that determine who you are, who you are will never change, nor does it determine your altitude of success. It's what's inside of you and what you allow God to do with the inside that enables him to exalt you with those talents that he placed inside of you. Read this poem and engraft its concepts into your spirit and you will be esteemed.

As I pass through this life, sometimes frowning, often clowning with smile in place, on a stage full of actors who all hide behind a different face. Each hope the real will not be traced, therefore remain distant from other's embrace. But there is a trail which leads to a story untold, it's found through the eye's the mirror of the soul. Mirrors which lead to chambers of a heart so cold, it must be warmed that it might unfold.

Though tainted by sin, there is treasure within, waiting for new life to begin,

He who searches the hearts of mortal men, is waiting outside for you to let him in.

You can live life without theatrics, stage fright and acceptance tactics.

Be who God created you to be, no longer held captive behind the wrong personality.

Look into the mirror and see the eyes that reflect your soul, can you see a story yet untold? Have you placed the old you upon a shelf? Do you find it difficult just being yourself?

What are your fears, is it your peers? At this stage of life are you looking for cheers? Unleash the real, let it not be concealed, don't hold back no matter what the worldly appeal.

Come out of your cage; step out on the stage as yourself portrayed,

Life is too short to be called on some roster, only to find out that you weren't yourself just an Imposter.

WHAT WE CAN AND CAN'T DO

We as human beings need to recognize our limitations. It's not about what we can do, but what God can do through us. Without him we are very limited, with him we are unlimited because he is omnipotent. Although God has given mankind the ability to do amazing things such as create spaceships that will fly to the moon, or develop probes that will penetrate deep into space and even land on Mars. We must not forget that without God unveiling scientific knowledge and information to mankind and expanding his understanding, man would still be getting whiplash riding five spoke chariots.

This poem is a reminder to me that man is mortal and God immortal, man is limited and God unlimited. But with God, we can do all things.

We can speak eloquently, with words sounding good to the ear,

And write lyrics that will beckon your held back tears.

We can even create instruments that will play beautiful tunes,

And determine how many days until the next eclipse of the moon.

And we can build ships that will sail the seven seas,

And frame mansions out of the finest cedar trees.

And We can build great towers like the stratosphere,

And design rockets that will burst through our atmosphere.

But we can't change the circuits of the wind, and calm a raging see,

Nor can we rotate the sun back ten or more degree's.

Nor can we create a star or cause the dead to awake,

Or shake the heavens with thunder, or make the earth quake.

But I know there is one who can, who filled the earth with springs,

His name is Jesus the alpha and omega, the infinite King of kings.

It is He, who formed the earth and fearfully created you,

So let him tell you what you can or can not do.

CREATIONS FORMAT

Did you know that everything in the known and unknown universe was not haphazardly designed? It did not evolve nor did God just over time alter what already preexisted with no preplanned purpose. Everything has a purpose and a reason and was designed to simulate something connected with future spiritual events. When God laid down the format of creation in his mind, He did it with a future glory in mind.

Romans 1:20-21 (For the invisible things of him from the creation of the world are clearly seen, being understood by the things that are made, even his eternal power and Godhead; so that they are without excuse: Because that, when they knew God, they glorified him not as God, neither were thankful; but became vain in their imaginations, and their foolish heart was darkened.)

Agnosticism entered the mind of vain men who like to argue against the truth; men with thoughts that lead to a deep abyss of fruitless Ideas; like evolution and reincarnation. They knew of God and believed in a higher power but would argue against God to sound intelligent to men eventually leading to their reprobation, where their hearts were darkened, and they began to deny the very existence of God, believing what they first only debated. But that never changed the reality of God's ultimate plan.

God loved the idea that he would not be alone in this beautiful universe. Just as you and I get lonely, God remained in solitude for an inexplicable amount of time. It was in this state that God came up with a preliminary design for creation. Now get this, God's creation was perfect, every spirit in heaven, every molecular element, every herb, mammal, and creature upon the face of the earth and in the depths of the sea. God also in his foreknowledge (his ability to look into the future) knew that when he created man; that man would fall (be challenged and tempted by the Devil and fall from a state of righteousness by being disobedient to God's orders, and yielding to the bad advice and lies of Satan.) Now does this make man an imperfect creation? Not at all and I will explain why and how I ascertained this insight.

You see <u>God so loved the world.</u> Meaning, God loved his creation in its entirety, but most of all mankind for which he created the habitation for. But for love to be true and perfect it cannot be altered or placed under forced perimeters or under a dictatorship. Now love places safety perimeters but does not force them to be obeyed. It allows the loved to respond in love of their own will. It must be free and willing to love, not forced. God gave a perfectly designed man, (body, soul, and spirit) a freewill to love him back by being obedient to his safety perimeters: Knowing that God's perimeters would protect man from another force and spiritual hierarchy that man at the time was totally ignorant of; the Devil. Now this is the love God had for man and this is the very love that God wanted man to have for him, which included trust and loyalty. Therefore, in God's creation of the earth, everything that was created was designed with the purpose to instruct man and teach man more about God and his power. This is why people are still in awe of things created to this present day.

The earth and heavens were also created as a pictorial of the predetermined plan of redemption for fallen man. Such as the sun setting representing death, the dawning representing the resurrection; the bridegroom coming out of His chamber (Psalms 19:5). Plants falling to the earth shedding seeds that rise with new life, Death of all creatures, and birth of new beings representing perpetual life. God being all-powerful and all-knowing created the world and the heavens, knowing that man would fail when faced with curiosity because he is not God and he has the desire to know all things like his creator, Yet God knew it would be unhealthy for him mentally to know all things as He does because he would think he is equivalent to his creator. Man is so curious about everything, why I can't touch that, why I can't have this, and will justify his reasons for having it even if he knows deep within his heart that it is contrary to God's ways. Recognize that God's creation is perfect without your opinion as to what you think it should be, and that you should Learn of Him so that you would understand His creation. (Matthew 11:29 Take my yoke upon you and learn of me, for I am meek and lowly and you shall find rest unto your souls.)

Spoke Into Existence

Just think, the mere words of God are so powerful that things appear at the sound of His voice. With one command the entire universe as we know it materialized. All forms of life within it carry a molecular structure. All DNA contains a structure embedded within it of what it shall become. To say that we evolved is to say that somehow an explosion took place and took on a miraculous beautiful form of life. This is ludicrous and discredits the supernatural designer God. The designer duplicates these molecular structures with unique differences. What I mean by duplicate is to make another kind after its kind yet make it different and unique. Thus, meaning if it evolved it would change its DNA structure. Yet each being has a totally different DNA pattern but not structure, meaning it will be what it is whether dog or cat yet different stripes, spots, and sizes. It would be virtually impossible for two beings to be one and the same for each would contain their own mind, will, and emotions, different soul and spirit though they appear identical.

This tells that a supernatural designer is designing unique creatures, beings, and plant life. To the common eye, there may appear to be no difference, but the supernatural designer can find all the differences including the speed of growth due to the amount of light and proper nourishment based on different soils, The environment and air quality, God knows an infinite number of infinities, he knows the very number of hairs on your head, and not one can fall to the ground without his knowledge and or approval. We are thus limited in our capacity to understand the depth of the creator. <u>Isaiah 55:8-9 (For my thoughts are not your thoughts, neither are your ways my ways, saith the Lord. For as the heavens are higher than the earth, so are my ways higher than your ways, and my thoughts than your thoughts)</u>. No two humans think exactly alike on all issues, for all have been through different experiences that formed their opinions. Pain toleration, and emotional strengths, all have their braking points.

To give a first-place award to a second-place runner up is to deprive the first-place winner of his victory. To give credit to evolution for all creation is to deprive the true creator of his glory. DNA is intellect in a cell. It's programmed to become what it will eventually become. Who placed that intellect there? The programmer God.

Evolution is like saying the residue of an explosion was suddenly programmed by electric impulses to for a living creature. What are the chances of that? And what are the chances of it doing it thousands of times over again to form several thousand different creatures that balance one another out? Virtually impossible and unrealistic. Only a fool would believe that. Maybe that's why the Bible says a fool says there is no God.

The Bible says in Genesis chap.1 and 2 that God created all life forms and placed man in dominion over the earth. What has changed over the last six thousand years? Who still has dominion? Who has tamed whales how to jump out of the water on command, who tamed lions to jump through hoops, who has taught birds to retrieve and carry messages across the globe? Who has sent space shuttles into space, has a monkey? Humans. The Bible confirms creation by a supernatural creator who designed humans and creatures to think and know their roles. Why defy all truth and biblical wisdom and knowledge? You only become a liar and the truth will always remain. Philosophies come and go, but all truth remains. Theories have changed over the years, but the truth of God's word and what it declares is infallible, inerrant, and impeccable.

Man in his desire to be true has made himself a liar through his vain philosophies. In his effort to be exalted and esteemed a man of wisdom, he has become a fool. Only a fool says a baker didn't bake a cake; the batter suddenly amalgamated and mixed when an explosion of eggs, sugar, flour, salt, milk, and baking powder fell into a pan, slid itself into an oven already placed on 350 degrees. This is equivalent to saying an explosion took place and created billions of unique life forms on land and in the sea, and only a fool would believe in such ignorant hypotheses or assumptions.

I would rather believe that God spoke it into existence because he is Omnipotent and all-powerful. And only an omniscient God can know enough to create such a wonderful work of art.

ADOLESCENTS

      We often regret what we have done in our adolescent years. But now we have the chance to make a change. Don't wait until you're in jail to decide to wise up. This is from someone who knows and has been there. In this poem I speak of the consequences of waiting until you have nowhere else to turn but to look out the window of a prison saying, when I get out, I'll do it right next time.

As I stared out the window, watching the moon 'twas crescent,

Reminiscing of the times when I was a young adolescent.

My peers, some had fathers, some like me grew up without,

As we got older, some joined gangs, others took another route.

A few died along the way living lives most uncouth,

They never thought for one minute, they'd be cut down in their youth.

Sometimes we take chances and our life for granted,

Not realizing in our children the seeds we planted.

What we have done in modesty, they do in excess,

We quiz them on life, when we failed to pass the test.

Experience taught me things, I couldn't have otherwise ascertained,

Unfortunately, it was later, now I stare out my prison window pane.

Still looking back in retrospect, with the crescent moon still glaring,

Wanting to erase the past of this weight I'm still bearing.

I could only pray and lay this heavy burden down,

And wait till my release date comes round.

But I know I will have a second chance to live as I should,

That people will not fear, as I reenter my old neighborhood.

TIME CONTINUES ON

12/13/08.

      Have you noticed that time doesn't stand still for nobody but God? Only God turns time back by moving the sun ten degrees. But life inevitably goes on no matter what we do. You sleep and wake up and it's a new day, meaning the time continued even when you were asleep. We clock in and clock out when our time is done on the job, but time doesn't stop even though you clock out, that just stops the money flow. We will clock in this life and clock out of it as well. The Bible says your life is like a vapor. Look back and think of how many people you know have left this earth in the past ten years. I pondered how fast time went by, remembering when my kids were just babies and now, they are teens. This poem depicts a course of time for each of us to reflect on. Tell me did time continue?

Time moves on when all else stands still,

Whether we are young, ill or over the hill.

Time continues on.

Like and hourglass as the sand seeps through,

Each grain is like death approaching you.

Time continues on.

We mortals live until life cease,

We parlay but the graveyards feast.

Cause time continues on.

We struggle, hustle, and move with haste,

Wondering when we depart who'll take our place.

Cause time continues on.

What will you do to make your time count?

Do you live by faith or fear and doubt?

Cause time continues on.

All you've done, the good and bad,

Would you say it made you happy or sad?

While your thinking, Time continues on.

THE BROKEN RIBBON

One day I decided I was going to type. This was when they still used regular typewriters that required ink ribbons. As I began to put the ink ribbon cartridge in the typewriter, it slipped out of my hand falling to the floor, it shattered. So, I got down on my knees to pick up all the pieces, finding every piece I tried to reassemble the ribbon. Struggling, making no progress due to lack of knowledge of how the pieces went, in frustration I was just about to throw the ribbon into the trash when a kindhearted gentleman walked up to lend a helping hand. With a smile he said, "Don't this belong here on top, referring to the placement of the ribbon. He knew exactly how to reassemble the ribbon and even carried spare parts. Now I could have been stubborn and refused his help, but I humbled myself and let him take control. Shortly later the ribbon was back in use, and I resumed working.

The good thing was he didn't even charge me a thing and I didn't have to buy another ribbon because I didn't have the money.

Our lives were like that ribbon; broken, shattered because of sin. Our future hopes and dreams seemed to just slip out of our hands and fall apart. Just like the prodigal son, prodigal living took its toll, then god walked up to take control. Speaking through a kindhearted servant of his, he offered you a helping hand. He had plenty of spare parts and was only looking to help you put your life back together. Did you refuse? Are you still struggling on your own trying to put your own life back together? (There is a way which seemeth right unto a man, but the end thereof is the way of death. Proverbs 14:12.) The reason why you can't put your own life back together is because you don't know how the pieces go, only God does. The word of God is the instructional booklet on broken lives, and Jesus Christ is the physician who does the operation. Accept Him as your Lord and Savior and he will restore your broken heart, soul, mind, and spirit to good health. Then you can be used like that ribbon. And it won't cost you a thing.

THE LOST NATION

Our nation was founded on Christianity and now we can't pray in schools or even mention Jesus Christ unless we refer to him in a historic manner. We are now defending against civil unions to keep the sanctity of marriage. And Oh how foolish we are to war and fight over land, when there is sufficient amount for everyone. Yet we toil and hoard heaps of oil, gold, silver, and many other perishable things, yet the soul of man stands in jeopardy due to greed. When are we going to wake up and smell the fragrance of love? He that loveth not knoweth not God for God is love, yet we hate, we kill and we destroy in the name of God and religion. We have things twisted. Know ye not that it is the devil that came to rob, kill, and destroy, it doesn't take much thought to know where we get it from. But God came so that we might have life and life more abundantly. Therefore if you claim to believe

In God, you should believe in life not death, not war. So where cometh wars and fighting's among you? Come they not hence, even of your lust that war in your members, ye lust and have not: ye kill and desire to have, and cannot obtain: ye fight and war, yet ye have not: because ye ask not. (Not Correctly) ye ask and receive not because ye ask amiss (Evil, badly, wickedly). That ye may consume it upon your lust. Lust is covetousness, covetousness is idolatry. We are worshiping land, money, gold, silver, and other material things over the life of another. We claim we are heirs of the land, and yet we die and leave it to another greedy person. Family feuding, fighting and separating over a dead person's hat or coat. Where is our compassion and love for one another? The enemy is one very near, in fact so near you can't even see him until you look in the mirror. You face the enemy every day and think he is your friend. It is you, the opposite of love, the opposite of God. If you want to get rid of the real enemy, get rid of the hate and envy in your heart. Love is your friend, love is the principal thing, for love brings peace, and hate brings war. Love brings respect. It is love that created all things and it is the love for things that is destroying all things. Our nation is imploding due to greed and selfishness. We have ignored the two greatest commandments, to love the Lord God with all our heart, soul, mind, and strength, and to love our neighbor as ourselves. And even if you don't love God, love yourself and others for we are created in his image. And if you love yourself, you must love God's creation. Therefore, let love be your guide, let peace be at your side. And we will no longer be a lost nation.

LORD WHAT YOU ARE TO ME

What is God to you? How do you describe his attributes? Many people in this world don't have a clue about who or what God is. Paul the apostle told the Athenians; who would just spend their time in nothing Else, but to tell or hear some new thing, Paul the apostle said for in him we live, and move and have our being; as certain also of your own poets have said, for we are also his offspring. For they had an altar with an inscription; TO THE UNKNOWN GOD. Unknown because they didn't know who God was. God is not a gold or silver item graven by the crafty artwork of a man's device. He is the omnipotent, all-powerful God of the universe who supplies our every need. This poem describes just a little bit of what God is to me.

Lord, you're the humility to the meek, the strength to the weary and weak, the whole to the broken and incomplete, the victor and the commander of Satan's defeat. Lord, you're the comprehension of our understanding, the reason why we're standing, the life we're apprehending, the thread used in our hearts mending. Lord, you're the calm in the midst of the storm, the comfort in the times when we mourn, the apparel of which we are spiritually adorned, the sole reason why we're re-born. Lord you're the joy counted in tribulations, the hope of our salvation, our source of overcoming temptations, the delight of our conversations. Lord, you're the way out of this earthly test, the guide of our spiritual quest, the confidence built when we acquiesce, the healer, best of the best. Lord, you're the foundation of which we stand, the only begotten Son of man, the reason why we can, the one whose second-coming is at hand. Lord, you're the only one in whom I trust, you formed man from the elements of dust, consisting of our earth's crust, why people sing in a melodious chorus.

LORD, YOU SMILE AT ME

God smiles at us in various ways that we tend to overlook. And if we open our eyes, we will see that God is smiling. Therefore, let everything that has breath praise the Lord.

Lord, you smile at me in the springtime, when the harvest is just breaking through, Lord you smile at me in the falltime, when the harvest is plentiful and due. Lord, you smile at me when the sun shines and the heat keeps me warm through the night. Oh Lord, you smile at me in these hard times when my trials seem to have blinded my sight. Lord, you smile at me through the flowers that blossom in full array. You smile at me when the sun comes up and dawns at the breaking of day. Lord, you smile at me through the spirit you breathe, which sustains my living soul. You smile at me to make me believe that your goodness has made me whole.

THE WEIGHT OF A DREAM

Some people have asked the question, where do dreams come from?
I've even asked the question once or twice. Well, the Bible says dreams come from the multitude of business, (worldly affairs) Affairs being the cares of life that we entangle ourselves in or are in pursuit of. When I examine my dreams, they come from suppressed fantasies or fears. Now a fantasy we consider a dream, but the things that we fear are nightmares. Sometimes dreams compel us to desire to go back to sleep. Some superstitious people believe that if you dream a dream three times it will come true. This fallacy is not true, although some may have experienced such rare co-incidents. But if you give your cares and worries to God, for he says to cast your cares upon him for he cares for you. Your dreams will be few and far between.

I've dreamed of mountain tops,

touching the early morning dew,

soaring like an eagle,

over the beautiful seacoast blue.

I've drifted into space,

touched sparkling gleaming stars,

landed on foreign planets,

and even visited the mystic of Mars.

I've dreamed of a land of peace,

where love fills the land,

people living in perfect harmony,

willing to lend a helping hand.

The land was void of poverty,

and all had equal shares,

but this was just a dream,

and then came the daunting nightmares.

Death was in the air,

seemed to be drawing near,

and wondered if it was calling my name,

'twas whispering in my ear.

I was running and hiding,

but couldn't evade death's face,

suddenly I awoke in ought to avoid its embrace.

I opened my Bible and turned to Psalm 23,

and there in those dark hours,

I found my peace and serenity.

Knew nightmares were afflictions,

brought on by principalities,

and a dream is just a dream,

not the essence of reality.

THEIR GOING TO LIVE WITH ME

For the joy that was set before him, he endured the cross despising the shame. What was the joy that was set before him? The joy was the fact that he would reconcile us back to God and we would live forever with him in glory. Jesus said in my Father's house there are many mansions, if it were not so I would have told you. He also said that he was going to prepare us a place. That means he is excited about the arrangement and reservation that we made when we accepted him as our Lord and Savior. I was lying on my bed in despair, feeling so alone and neglected. It was then the Holy Spirit came to comfort me letting me know how God reserved a place in heaven just for me. Just for me!!! Wow, even though I wasn't feeling special The Ultimate God and King of the universe took time to prepare a place just for me. If God were to write a poem this is what I believe it would say.

Their going to live with me, for all eternity,

Their going to live with me, in peace and tranquility.

There will be no weeping, no slumber or sleeping,

Just joyful reaping, and heavenly banquet feasting.

Their going to live with me in royal apparel,

They will join the angels in heavenly carols.

When the time comes for me to appear,

I will call and all my children will hear.

Their going to live with me, for all eternity,
Their going to live with me in my fraternity.
Oh I prepared a place for them in my palace,
For they sanctified themselves from sin and malice.
In the end we will join hands, all in one union,
And as a family partake of my heavenly communion.

They will be dressed in white for they fought the good fight,
And in my name Jesus they found power and might.
Don't be left behind and miss the blessing I designed,
Come while there is still time for your name to be signed.

Do you want to live with me, for all eternity?
Do you want to join my holy fraternity?
Your inheritance will not fade, only obey,
Now is the time for salvation so do not delay.

I offer you shelter from harm your storm will calm,
So place your trust in Jesus he's holding out his arm.
You're going to live with me forever in my kingdom,
I'm going to fill you with an abundance of my wisdom.

That's why in my image you were created,
To appear like me when your finally translated.
You're going to live with me for all eternity,
So come and join this holy fraternity.

IT IS MY DESIRE TO KNOW YOU

    I asked myself, what do I know about God? And it dawned on me that I didn't know enough. God is too immense, He's omnipotent, immutable, omniscient, omnipresent, loving, and kind, so how much did I know about him? I must say, not enough. Many of us say that we know God but do we really? How many of us even desire to know Him? Well, if you desire to know God there are a few basic things you need to do. For one he said draw nearer to him and he will draw nearer to you. He said behold he stands at the door of your heart waiting for you to open up so he can come in and commune with you and enlighten you on who he is. We then must consecrate ourselves by withdrawing from sinful and ungodly activities such as the bible indicates in Galatians 5. It is then and only then that the Lord makes his acquaintance with you.

1 Corinthians 6:14, 17-18 says; be ye not unequally yoked together with unbelievers, for what fellowship hath righteousness with unrighteousness, and what communion hath light with darkness. (So, if you're walking in darkness there is no possible way you can know God.) wherefore come out from among them and be ye separate saith the Lord, and touch not the unclean thing, and I will receive you, and be a father unto you and ye shall be my sons and daughters saith the Lord almighty.

The Lord is saying the only time He will make himself known to us or show that father-daughter relationship is when we stop doing what the world does. Going to clubs and getting our groove on, fornicating, committing adultery, lying, stealing, and everything that separates us from the straight and narrow. When we choose to be obedient and walk in God's word, God begins to make himself known to us, illuminating our spiritual eyes and enhancing our understanding, endowing us with the wisdom of his word. The hidden truths of his word become revealed and you begin to know the true riches that God has in store for you. Get to know God in your own special way. Draw near to him in prayer, and fellowship in his word and with his peculiar people. Herein is a song that glorifies God and implores him to manifest himself to you.

Lord as I read your love letter,

 my desire was to know you better.

For many years I felt so alone,

didn't know you were there but I should have known.

It was not you, it was me,

I was the one who was blind and could not see,

But then you came along to be my friend,

You told me you would be there until the end.

So I'm here Lord, please hold my hand

Take me to that promise land.

Lord I will do what you say do.

Cause it's my desire to know you.

Chorus: Lord I desire to know you better,

Lord I desire to know you better,

You've been by my side so faithfully,

You've waited so patiently.

Now I'm ready to learn of you,

So do to my heart what you said you would do.

I thought I knew you at one point in time,

But I found out latter it was only in my mind.

I desired you to show me a spiritual sign,

Like the wise men, when they saw that star shine.

I just want to see if you were real,

I wanted you to be revealed.

But now I know the reason why Jesus died,

So I could feel his spirit living on the inside.

INFUSE ME WITH STRENGTH

      This song declares my desire to receive strength from the lord to cope with the turmoil of the present times. We so often go through life on our own, trying to accomplish things in our own power. This only leads to utter failure. The Bible says in all your ways acknowledge him and he will direct your path. Let the Holy Spirit lead you and fill you with strength and you will never fail.

(Chorus) Infuse me with strength to carry on,

When I am weak then you are strong.

Though there may be trials throughout my day,

Help me dear Lord to yield to your way.

I often fell burdened, so faint within,

From the pressures of this body of sin.

But each day your light has shined upon me,

And from this burden you set me free.

I bow in your presence to offer praise,

For you are worthy, so my hands I raise.

Lift up my soul, that I might testify,

There's no other god in whom we can rely.

Fill me with your spirit; I need your power,

These times demand your filling hour to hour.

Infuse me with strength for my weary soul,

I'll no longer be broken but made fully whole.

WHEN YOU DIE, WHAT LIFE FORM WILL YOU BE?

Oh so often I hear people saying they will be reincarnated or take on some other life form. Saying they will come back as a rabbit or bird. I say I hope not because they will end up in a rotisserie thinking they are in hell from the fire on someone's grill lol. For the most part, they are totally unsure of the afterlife. The Bible doesn't fully say, but it does say, that it doth not yet appear what we shall be: but we know that when Jesus Christ shall appear, we shall be like him; for we shall see him as he is. And everyone who hath this hope in him purifies himself, even as he is pure.

Ask yourself, when you die what life form will you be,

Celestial or terrestrial, is there a consciousness to some degree.

Do you believe in life after death, once you breathe your last breath?

When ashes turn to ashes, will your soul be laid to rest?

Is the spirit world a reality or mans only hopeful created fiction,

Filled with fantasies of a paradise with an exaggerated description.

Or could it be the final state of existence, is there fear and doubt,

What is the root of your resistance, is it your only way out?

There are those who died and claim to have seen the light,

Then as they resuscitated professed the Bible was right.

Could this have been a self induced illusion of the mind?

Or a warning from God who decided to show a spiritual sign?

Just think who could have designed the world in the beauty of creation,

Does the seen reflect the unseen; if so what is there relation?

Only God could have created such a spectrum of radiant sights,

Scientist scope the extent of the galaxies beautiful luminous lights.

The heavens declare the glory of God; can not fathom his awesome power,

He spoke the world into existence and arrayed it with colorful flowers.

The Bible says after death like angels we will be conceived,

And through Jesus Christ and eminent state of life will be received.

I hold dear, most sincere, to this system of belief,

What other faith offers a hope of life eternal exempt form grief?

Imagine a place filled with love, no doubt what you will be,

Majestic like angels, with heaven as your final destiny.

REMEMBER ME

    I was reminiscing about the thief on the cross, who told the Lord to remember him. We're always asking the Lord to remember us, so why not flip that around by remembering him? Just as the scripture says, remember the Lord in the days of your youth, before the evil days come, when you say you have no pleasure in them. How often do we go through life doing our own thing, pleasing ourselves? We lie recumbent when it is incumbent upon us to serve God now while we live. God's goals for our lives, we soon forget, due to complacency and spiritual amnesia: As Paul would say carnality. Christ has commissioned us, and oh how we forget what he delegated to us, The gospel and the gospel way of living.

REMEMBER CHRIST BY REMEMBERING OTHERS

      Jesus said what you have done to the least of these you've done unto him. So if you forget about others you're forgetting about him. Remember how he died for you so that you could live in paradise? Paradise was not just for you but for others too. What if the one who shared the gospel with you neglected to dispense the good news to you? Where would you be going?

Romans 10:9-13 says, for whosoever shall call upon the name of the Lord shall be saved. How then shall they hear without a preacher? And who shall they preach, except they be sent? As it is written, how beautiful are the feet of them that carry the gospel of peace and being good tidings of good things? Now do you remember why Jesus commissioned us to preach the gospel (Good news)? How else will they hear it? This is how we remember Jesus Christ by departing good tidings to those God brings our way. Not just by partaking of the elements in the Lord's supper. Otherwise, with whom would we take it if the gospel was not preached? Nobody would be saved to partake in it. Therefore, once again I say, remember the Lord Jesus Christ by remembering others.

IN TIMES OF TROUBLE

What do you do in times of trouble? Go get a gun, call the homeboys or home girls? Do you run to Mom and Dad and ask for help, who is the first person you call on? Many times I just try to figure a way out of my situation but often my way is never God's way. My way had me incarcerated. Herein I write to you to tell you the most effective way. Why not go to the one who has the power to change your circumstances? The Lord has all power and can take whatever predicament and turn it into a powerful testimony. I wrote this song as I was reflecting on God's goodness in my times of trouble. If you are in trouble, call on the Lord, he is Jehovah our provider.

In times of trouble, Lord you have given me,

The answers to life, when life is a mystery.

When I was weary, and overwhelmed by the enemy,

I went forth to sweet victory cause your hands on me.

Lord in the time of trouble, when my world seem to go under,

It was hard to keep my head up till you showed me your wonders.

I felt your Holy Spirit fill me with might and power,

Though I was feeble you became my strong tower.

I'm going to keep pressing, to receive my blessing,

Let patience have its perfect work, as I endure this testing.

The devil thought I was defeated, when my mind became corrupt,

But a righteous man falls seven times but always gets back up.

The battle is over, when God raised up his only Son

The victory has been clamed and Jesus Christ has won.

So through these times of trouble, I've grown bolder,

I'm in the Lords army now and I'm a good soldier.

When you think its time to acquiesce, stand where Jesus stood,

That's why troubles never fade me, I know there only for my good.

Do you want to come with me? I'm going up yonder,

The road is narrow and there's no room to wander.

MODEL OF A MAN

    Today in this society, men think they are men because they have been through puberty or have little facial hair. But being a man is so much more than physical development or reaching physical maturity. Now don't get me wrong, a man is a man when he reaches physical maturity, but a model of a man deals with his total essence, his mind, will, and emotions.

How does he respond when faced with adversity? How does he respond when tribulations come his way, will he respond like a man or a child, will his rationality be lacking development? Will he reason and weigh the cost from beginning to end? Being a man is more than just a physical thing, it has to be the whole being of man. (1 Corinthians 13:11 Paul the apostle said, "When I was a child, I spoke as a child, I understood as a child, I thought as a child: but when I became <u>a man,</u> I put away childish things".) Today men are still acting as a child, thinking as a child, and understanding as a child. They neglect to take responsibility as a man and become wasteful, deadbeat, And careless. A model of a man is honored by both God and man. So be a model of a man. Emulate the man I depict in this poem.

A model of a man carries himself with dignity,

Firm in all he believes.

His character traits are witty,

And criticism he willingly receives.

Loyal to all in his union,

Faithful throughout the end.

Love, joy and peace is his religion,

When praised he condescends.

His strength rest within his faith,

Though he weeps, think not a weakness,

For this is his strongest trait,

A character they call meekness.

He endures tribulation with spirituality,

He's known all throughout the land.

Turns dreams in to reality,

For he's a model of a man.

Though trials come he perseveres,

Knowing tribulations worketh patience,

Tenacity up rises within his soul,

To overcome fleshly sensations.

And when all is said and done,

He rises to the occasion,

And for a model of a man,

He deserves a standing ovation.

MODEL OF A WOMAN

What people call a model of a woman today is either a 5'11 or more diva strutting her way on a modeling runway or a businesswoman; one who has taken the independence of a man and has adorned themselves on the outward yet the inward being is left characterless. It is this kind of woman who has often forsaken her role as a mother or helpmeet. Now the same goes for a woman as I once said of a man. There is a godly standard in scripture for a woman. Proverbs 31:30 says: favor is deceitful, and beauty is vain: but a woman that feareth the Lord, she shall be praised. Read all of Proverbs 31 it speaks of a virtual woman. This poem depicts the model of a woman and her virtues. Will you be a model of a woman?

A model of a woman is not concerned with outward beauty,

Her adorning is of the heart, follows her God given duty.

She reaches forth her hand to the poor, with compassionate pity,

She fears the Lord and cares for those who are neglected in her city.

She builds her house with joy, and elevates it by praise,

She teaches younger woman to learn her godly ways.

With the work of her hands, she cause things to flourish,

She makes sure that all in her home is blessed and well nourished.

She's gifted and bares many God given talents,

Without her in the world men would have no balance.

She's filled with the spirit, prudent and kindhearted,

She humbly receives praise but all flattery is disregarded.

She's crowned with wisdom, and her words all have merit,

She's hospitable; when she's blessed she is willing to share it.

She's what you want in your life, one to entrust your baby,

She's a model of a woman, a beautiful wonderful lady.

THE PAST

I know it's hard to put the past behind you when everyone keeps bringing it up. We cannot truly learn to forgive others until we learn to forgive ourselves. If God can cast our sins as far as the East is from the West why can't we? Read this poem.

They say put your past behind you, and just go on about your way,

But somehow my past keeps popping up, and carried into the next given day.

They say let by gone be by gone, or why don't you sweep it under the rug,

But like a painting covers a hole in the wall, it's still there waiting to be plugged.

I try to let water stay under the bridge, but fishermen cease not to cast,

Often pulling up big memory fish, that once was a part of the past.

I heard a voice saying; I'm the alpha and omega the first and last,

I'm the God who holds the future; I bless your present and blot out your past.

IT'S AMAZING

When I think of all God has done it baffles my understanding, God is truly amazing. We cannot fathom his power or begin to understand how mere words created matter. The sights of the universe are breathtaking and mind-boggling. Just imagine how the earth and planets maintain their orbit, how the sun heats the earth and gives it light in the day and the moon at night. Just the mere thought of this compelled me to write this song.

Vs 1:

It's amazing to me, how you keep the world going round and round yea,

It's amazing to me, how the sun keeps on shinning, and the moon gives its glare.

It's amazing to me how you didn't say a word when they treated you unfair,

It's amazing to me, the way you gave your live just to show you care.

Chorus:

Oh Lord, your amazing, So amazing, That's why your name forever I'm praising, my hands I'm raising, cause your so amazing, oh Lord yes you are amazing, so amazing, So far beyond my imagination, my consolation, strength in temptation, your so amazing, So amazing to me..

Vs 2:

It's amazing to me how you know when I'm down and in despair,

It's amazing to me how I call on your name and you're always there.

Its amazing to me Lord how I pray to you and you answer my prayer.

Oh it's amazing to me cause no other love can even compare.

Repeat Chorus:

Vs. 3:

It's amazing to me how you tell the sea to stay and it heeds your decree,

It's amazing to me how you rose from the dead just to give us the victory.

It's amazing to me how a God so strong can live inside of me,

It's amazing to me cause I was bound in chains but you set me free.

Vs 4:

It's amazing to me, how beautiful it is when clouds fill the sky,

It's amazing to me, how the rain falls down from way on high,

It's amazing to me, how the wind blows, and birds rise to fly.

It's amazing to me, Cause your loves so strong, it cant be denied.

Good Morning Jesus

When we wake up in the morning, God is always there, do you say good morning to him? He is worthy of it; he is the one who made it good. He woke you up one more day, gave you one more chance to live, one more chance to achieve excellence. No matter what your situation is, or your circumstance, it is a good morning because it could always be worse. I wrote this song thinking about praising him in the morning on Sunday worship. How good it would be to just sing a good morning song to the Lord of Lords and the Kind of Kings. Oh, good morning Jesus.

Good morning Jesus, thank you for another day,

Another day to praise you, as we go along the way.

Good morning Jesus, for another chance to pray,

That you supply our every need, so I do not go astray.

Oh good morning precious Jesus, Show me what to say,

To every unbeliever, who you bring across my way.

Good morning lovely Jesus, mold me like potters clay,

Deliver me from the evil one, that like you I might portray.

Chorus:

Oh, Oh, Oh Jesus, this morning I dedicate to worship and praise,

I'm going to sing my heart and soul to you with my hands upraised.

Oh, Oh, oh, good morning Jesus, you're the infinite end of days,

Every time you wake me up in the morning, your power is displayed.

Good morning blessed Jesus, give me the strength to do your will,

Let everything I say and do this day be blessed and spirit filled.

Good morning precious Jesus, your salvation is my shield,

Guide me enlighten me, so the world may know your real.

THE TREE THAT WITHERED

      Just think of the unlimited power of God displayed through Human flesh. Jesus showed how words have power. We say things and go on our merry way not knowing the power of our words. There was a tree that didn't bear any fruit. So basically, it wasn't serving the purpose of what it was created to do. Imagine buying an apple tree and planting it and it grows up to not bring forth any apples. You waited with happy anticipation of getting to make apple pie, apple juice, applesauce, but instead nothing but leaves to pick up during the fall season. What would you do? Well, Jesus cursed the tree just to show his disciples how he felt about believers not bearing any spiritual fruit. Believers only being caught up in the world living worldly lives, not leading anyone to Christ. Living life with no urgency. People walk past with their souls in jeopardy of being lost for all eternity. Well, this poem is about that tree. It's about you and me.

Seeds were planted long ago, to see what may arise,

Some came up to flourish while others withered and died.

Like those who came and went, only just passing by,

Never leaving anything behind and I wondered why.

Jesus came along one day, and saw a tree not bearing fruit,

Like all those who live life daily only to chase filthy loot.

He said a few words and the tree was cursed to die,

The disciples marveled cause it had when they next passed it by.

We have all been entrusted with a gift from up above.

But sometimes we get distracted and forget about Gods love.

How Christ came to die so we would not live corrupt.

Be free from sin and not strung out on drugs.

Remember the harvest is plentiful but the laborers are few.

If Jesus cursed a tree for no fruit, will he do that to you?

Or will he say well done my child you been faithful and true.

Come in to my kingdom your one of the chosen few.

WHAT CAME FIRST THE CHICKEN OR THE EGG?

I was in a debate about this very subject. But then I thought, I finally proved Creation over evolution. Every egg begins in a chicken. The rooster then fertilizes the egg of which in all creatures the male seed determines the gender. Then the egg must be incubated until it hatches.

From that point, the hen nurtures and protects the baby chick from dangerous elements such as predators and outside surroundings like rain,

Extreme heat and or cold. Imagine being born in the winter, life doesn't stop being produced in the winter or any season. And in some places in this world, it gets well below freezing. Every creature depends upon its father and mother to protect it and raise it until it can independently protect or feed itself. And there are so many species.

Why does every creature in this known universe have two genders except humans? Exactly because there are only two genders, male and female. The genders are determined based on the ability to reproduce, either you have female reproductive glands or male reproductive glands. This has nothing to do with what one feels like they are in their mind.

Only someone delusional in their mind can think they are a plane but try flying off a bridge. We all know what their fate would be. You can think you are a Lion but walk into a pride of lions and try and fit in. Think you are a fish and jump into the ocean with no gills I bet you drown. Be born with male genitalia and try to have a baby naturally. It's humanly impossible.

Because of humans' sinful deviant nature, these lucid perverted thoughts come. They plague our minds if we don't have something like a designer's manual to keep us on track. If something goes wrong with your computer, you need someone to reprogram the computer because you accidentally pressed the wrong button. They usually are familiar with how the computer was designed to function. In this case, God who made us knows how he designed us, so who are we to call ourselves anything other than what our genetics say we are?

Think about this, every creature created is in a fight for survival. We all battle the elements within the four seasons. Yet in this ecosystem every One of us depends upon one another to survive. Every tree drops seeds that dictate what it is. If an apple tree drops an apple seed to the ground, will that seed eventually germinate and bring forth Leons? I think not.

If I plant watermelon seeds, should I look forward to harvesting onions?

Of course not. This is because the DNA (Deoxyribonucleic acid) which speaks of structure determines what it will become. Basically, the format and design of what it will be. This is why they can determine who the parents are out of millions of people. I'm sure you've heard the apple doesn't fall far from the tree. This means a person inevitably shares similar traits as their parents.

The Bible is the best-selling book of all time for a reason.

It's used in archaeology, science, history ext. And is the only book that gives the actual account and order of creation. In Archaeology they've used it to find lost cities, validate the parting of the red sea, recent discoveries had Chines scientist locate Noah's Ark and they don't even believe in God. It also explains the continental divide. It also explains the Chicken being made before the egg.

Printed by Libri Plureos GmbH in Hamburg, Germany